Table of Contents

Executive Summary.. 1

1. Introduction and Background... 7
   a. Money Market Funds.. 7
   b. MMFs' Susceptibility to Runs.. 8
   c. MMFs in the Recent Financial Crisis... 11

2. The SEC's Changes to the Regulation of MMFs... 13
   a. SEC Regulatory Changes... 14
   b. Need for Further Reform to Reduce Susceptibility to Runs..................... 16

3. Policy Options for Further Reducing the Risks of Runs on MMFs................. 18
   a. Floating Net Asset Values.. 19
   b. Private Emergency Liquidity Facility for MMFs..................................... 23
   c. Mandatory Redemptions in Kind.. 25
   d. Insurance for MMFs... 26
   e. A Two-Tier System of MMFs, with Enhanced Protections for Stable NAV MMFs.. 29
   f. A Two-Tier System of MMFs, with Stable NAV MMFs Reserved for Retail Investors.. 30
   g. Regulating Stable NAV MMFs as Special Purpose Banks....................... 32
   h. Enhanced Constraints on Unregulated MMF Substitutes......................... 35

Executive Summary

Several key events during the financial crisis underscored the vulnerability of the financial system to systemic risk. One such event was the September 2008 run on money market funds (MMFs), which began after the failure of Lehman Brothers Holdings, Inc., caused significant capital losses at a large MMF. Amid broad concerns about the safety of MMFs and other financial institutions, investors rapidly redeemed MMF shares, and the cash needs of MMFs exacerbated strains in short-term funding markets. These strains, in turn, threatened the broader economy, as firms and institutions dependent upon those markets for short-term financing found credit increasingly difficult to obtain. Forceful government action was taken to stop the run, restore investor confidence, and prevent the development of an even more severe recession. Even so, short-term funding markets remained disrupted for some time.

The Treasury Department proposed in its *Financial Regulatory Reform: A New Foundation* (2009), that the President's Working Group on Financial Markets (PWG) prepare a report on fundamental changes needed to address systemic risk and to reduce the susceptibility of MMFs to runs. Treasury stated that the Securities and Exchange Commission's (SEC) rule amendments to strengthen the regulation of MMFs—which were in development at the time and which subsequently have been adopted—should enhance investor protection and mitigate the risk of runs. However, Treasury also noted that those rule changes could not, by themselves, be expected to prevent a run on MMFs of the scale experienced in September 2008. While suggesting a number of areas for review, Treasury added that the PWG should consider ways to mitigate possible adverse effects of further regulatory changes, such as the potential flight of assets from MMFs to less regulated or unregulated vehicles.

This report by the PWG responds to Treasury's call.[1] The PWG undertook a study of possible further reforms that, individually or in combination, might mitigate systemic risk by complementing the SEC's changes to MMF regulation. The PWG supports the SEC's recent actions and agrees with the SEC that more should be done to address MMFs' susceptibility to runs. This report details a number of options for further reform that the PWG requests be examined by the newly established Financial Stability Oversight Council (FSOC). These options range from measures that could be implemented by the SEC under current statutory authorities to broader changes that would require new legislation, coordination by multiple government agencies, and the creation of new private entities. For example, a new requirement that MMFs adopt floating net asset values (NAVs) or that large funds meet redemption requests in kind could be accomplished by SEC rule amendments. In contrast, the introduction of a private emergency liquidity facility, insurance for MMFs, conversion of MMFs to special purpose banks, or a two-tier system of MMFs that might combine some of the other measures likely would involve a coordinated effort by the SEC, bank regulators, and financial firms.

---

[1] The PWG (established by Executive Order 12631) is comprised of the Secretary of the Treasury (who serves as its Chairman), the Chairman of the Federal Reserve Board of Governors, the Chairman of the Securities and Exchange Commission, and the Chairman of the Commodity Futures Trading Commission.

Importantly, this report also emphasizes that the efficacy of the options presented herein would be enhanced considerably by the imposition of new constraints on less regulated or unregulated MMF substitutes, such as offshore MMFs, enhanced cash funds, and other stable value vehicles. Without new restrictions on such investment vehicles, which would require legislation, new rules that further constrain MMFs may motivate some investors to shift assets into MMF substitutes that may pose greater systemic risk than MMFs.

The PWG requests that the FSOC consider the options discussed in this report to identify those most likely to materially reduce MMFs' susceptibility to runs and to pursue their implementation. To assist the FSOC in any analysis, the SEC, as the regulator of MMFs, will solicit public comments, including the production of empirical data and other information in support of such comments. A notice and request for comment will be published in the near future. Following a comment period, a series of meetings will be held in Washington, D.C. with various stakeholders, interested persons, experts, and regulators.

MMFs are susceptible to runs

MMFs are mutual funds. They are investment vehicles that act as intermediaries between shareholders who desire liquid investments and borrowers who seek term funding. With nearly $3 trillion in assets under management, MMFs are important providers of credit to businesses, financial institutions, and governments. In addition, these funds are significant investors in some short-term funding markets.

Like other mutual funds, MMFs are regulated under the Investment Company Act of 1940 (ICA). In addition to ICA requirements for all mutual funds, MMFs must comply with SEC rule 2a-7, which permits these funds to maintain a stable net asset value (NAV) per share, typically $1. However, if the mark-to-market per-share value of a fund's assets falls more than one-half of 1 percent (to below $0.995), the fund must reprice its shares, an event colloquially known as "breaking the buck."

The events of September 2008 demonstrated that MMFs are susceptible to runs. In addition, those events proved that runs on MMFs not only harm fund shareholders, but may also cause severe dislocations in short-term funding markets that curtail short-term financing for companies and financial institutions and that ultimately result in a decline in economic activity. Thus, reducing the susceptibility of MMFs to runs and mitigating the effects of possible runs are important components of the overall policy goals of decreasing and containing systemic risks.

MMFs are vulnerable to runs because shareholders have an incentive to redeem their shares before others do when there is a perception that the fund might suffer a loss. Several features of MMFs, their sponsors, and their investors contribute to this incentive. For example, although a stable, rounded $1 NAV fosters an expectation of safety, MMFs are subject to credit, interest-rate, and liquidity risks. Thus, when a fund incurs even a small loss because of those risks, the stable, rounded NAV may subsidize shareholders who choose to redeem at the expense of the remaining shareholders. A larger loss that causes a fund's share price to drop below $1 per share (and thus break the buck) may prompt more substantial sudden, destabilizing redemptions. Moreover, although the expectations of safety fostered by the stable, rounded $1 NAV suggest parallels to an insured demand deposit account, MMFs have no formal capital buffers or insurance to prevent NAV declines; MMFs instead have relied historically on discretionary sponsor capital support to maintain stable NAVs. Accordingly, uncertainty about the availability of such support during crises may contribute to runs. Finally, because investors have come to view MMFs as extremely safe vehicles that meet all withdrawal requests on demand (and that are, in this sense, similar to banks), MMFs have attracted highly risk-averse investors who are particularly prone to flight when they perceive the possibility of a loss. These features likely mutually reinforce each other in times of crisis.

The SEC's new rules

In January 2010, the SEC adopted new rules for MMFs in order to make these funds more resilient and less likely to break the buck. The regulatory changes that mitigate systemic risks fall into three principal categories. First, the new rules enhance risk-limiting constraints on MMF portfolios by introducing new liquidity requirements, imposing additional credit-quality standards, and reducing the maximum allowable weighted average maturity of funds' portfolios. Funds also are required to stress test their ability to maintain a stable NAV. Second, the SEC's new rules permit a fund that is breaking the buck to suspend redemptions promptly and liquidate its portfolio in an orderly manner to limit contagion effects on other funds. Third, the new rules place more stringent constraints on repurchase agreements that are collateralized with private debt instruments rather than government securities.

The need for further measures

The SEC's new rules make MMFs more resilient and less risky and therefore reduce the likelihood of runs on MMFs, increase the size of runs that MMFs can withstand, and mitigate the systemic risks they pose. However, the SEC's new rules address only some of the features that make MMFs susceptible to runs, and more should be done to address systemic risk and the structural vulnerabilities of MMFs to runs. Indeed, the Chairman of the SEC characterized the new rules as "a first step" in strengthening MMFs, and Treasury's *Financial Regulatory Reform: A New Foundation* (2009) anticipated that measures taken by the SEC "should not, by themselves, be expected to prevent a run on MMFs of the scale experienced in September 2008."

Mitigating the risk of runs on MMFs is especially important because the events of September 2008 may have created an expectation that, in a future crisis, the government may provide support for MMFs at minimal cost in order to minimize harm to MMF investors, short-term funding markets, and the economy. Persistent expectations of unpriced government support distort incentives in the MMF industry and pricing in short-term funding markets, as well as heighten the systemic risk posed by MMFs. It is thus essential that MMFs be required to internalize fully the costs of liquidity or other risks associated with their operation.

In formulating reforms for MMFs, policymakers should aim primarily at mitigating systemic risk and containing the contagious effect that strains at individual MMFs can have on other MMFs and on the broad financial system. Importantly, preventing any individual MMF from ever breaking the buck is not a practical policy objective—though the new SEC rules for MMFs should help ensure that such events remain rare and thus constitute a limited means of containing systemic risk.

Policy options

The policy options discussed in this report may help further mitigate the susceptibility of MMFs to runs. Some of these options may be adopted by the SEC under its existing authorities. Others would require legislation and action by multiple government agencies and the MMF industry.

(a) Floating net asset values. A stable NAV has been a key element of the appeal of MMFs to investors, but a stable, rounded NAV also heightens funds' vulnerability to runs. Moving to a floating NAV would help remove the perception that MMFs are risk-free and reduce investors' incentives to redeem shares from distressed funds. However, the elimination of the stable NAV for MMFs would be a dramatic change for a nearly $3 trillion asset-management sector that has been built around the stable share price. Such a change may have several unintended consequences, including: (i) reductions in MMFs' capacity to provide short-term credit due to lower investor demand; (ii) a shift of assets to less regulated or unregulated MMF substitutes such as offshore MMFs, enhanced cash funds, and other stable value vehicles; and (iii) unpredictable investor responses as MMF NAVs begin to fluctuate more frequently.

(b) Private emergency liquidity facilities for MMFs. The liquidity risk of MMFs contributes importantly to their vulnerability to runs, and an external liquidity backstop to augment the SEC's new liquidity requirements for MMFs would help mitigate this risk. Such a backstop could buttress MMFs' ability to withstand outflows, internalize much of the liquidity protection costs for the MMF industry, offer efficiency gains from risk pooling, and reduce contagion effects. A liquidity facility would preserve fund advisers' incentives for not taking excessive risks because it would not protect funds from capital losses. As such, a liquidity facility alone may not prevent broader runs on MMFs triggered by concerns about widespread credit losses. Importantly, significant capacity, structure, pricing, and operational hurdles would have to be overcome to ensure that such a facility would be effective during crises, that it would not unduly distort incentives, and that it would not favor certain types of MMF business models.

(c) Mandatory redemptions in kind. When investors make large redemptions from MMFs, they may impose liquidity costs on other shareholders in the fund by forcing MMFs to sell assets in an untimely manner. A requirement that MMFs distribute large redemptions in kind, rather than in cash, would force these redeeming shareholders to bear their own liquidity costs and thus reduce the incentive to redeem. Depending on whether redeeming shareholders immediately sell the securities received, redemptions in kind may still generate market effects. Moreover, mandating redemptions in kind could present some operational and policy challenges. The SEC, for example, would have to make key judgments regarding when a fund must redeem in kind and how funds would fairly distribute portfolio securities.

(d) Insurance for MMFs. Treasury's Temporary Guarantee Program for Money Market Funds helped slow the run on MMFs in September 2008, and some form of insurance for MMF shareholders might be helpful in mitigating the risk of runs in MMFs. Unlike a private liquidity facility, insurance would limit credit losses to shareholders, so appropriate risk-based pricing would be critical in preventing insurance from distorting incentives, but such pricing might be difficult to achieve in practice. The appropriate scope of coverage also presents a challenge; unlimited coverage would likely cause large shifts of assets from the banking sector to MMFs, but limited insurance might do little to reduce institutional investors' incentives to run from distressed MMFs. The optimal form for insurance—whether it would be private, public, or a mix of the two—is also uncertain, particularly given the recent experience with private financial guarantees.

(e) A two-tier system of MMFs with enhanced protection for stable NAV funds. Reforms aimed at reducing MMFs' susceptibility to runs may be particularly effective if they permit investors to select the types of MMFs that best balance their appetite for risk and their preference for yield. Policymakers could allow two types of MMFs: stable NAV funds, which would be subject to enhanced protections such as, for example, required participation in a private liquidity facility or enhanced regulatory requirements; and floating NAV funds, which would have to comply with certain, but not all, rule 2a-7 restrictions (and which would presumably offer higher yields). Because this two-tier system would permit stable NAV funds to continue to be available, it would reduce the likelihood of a substantial decline in demand for MMFs and large-scale shifts of assets toward unregulated vehicles. At the same time, the forms of protection encompassed by such a system would mitigate the risks associated with stable NAV funds. It would also avoid problems that might be encountered in transitioning the entire MMF industry to a floating NAV. Moreover, during a crisis, a two-tier system might prevent large shifts of assets out of MMFs—and a reduction in credit supplied by the funds—if investors simply shift assets from riskier floating NAV funds toward safer (because of the enhanced protections) stable NAV funds. However, implementation of such a two-tier system would present the same challenges as the introduction of any individual enhanced protections (such as mandated access to a private emergency liquidity facility) that would be required for stable NAV funds, and the effectiveness of a two-tier system would depend on investors' understanding the risks associated with each type of fund.

(f) A two-tier system of MMFs with stable NAV MMFs reserved for retail investors. Another approach to the two-tier system already described could distinguish funds by investor type: Stable NAV MMFs could be made available only to retail investors, who could choose between stable NAV and floating NAV funds, while institutional investors would be restricted to floating NAV funds. The run on MMFs in September 2008 was almost exclusively due to redemptions from prime MMFs by institutional investors. Such investors typically have generated greater cash-flow volatility for MMFs than retail investors and have been much quicker to redeem MMF shares from stable NAV funds opportunistically. Hence, this approach would mitigate risks associated with a stable NAV by addressing the investor base of stable NAV funds rather than by mandating other types of enhanced protections for those funds. Such a system also would protect the interests of retail investors by reducing the likelihood that a run might begin in institutional MMFs (as it did in September 2008) and spread to retail

funds, while preserving the original purpose of MMFs, which was to provide retail investors with cost-effective, diversified investments in money market instruments. This approach would require the SEC to define who would qualify as retail and institutional investors, and distinguishing those categories will present challenges. In addition, a prohibition on sales of stable NAV MMFs shares to institutional investors may have several of the same unintended consequences as a requirement that all MMFs adopt floating NAVs (see option *(a)* in this section).

(g) Regulating stable NAV MMFs as special purpose banks. Functional similarities between MMF shares and bank deposits, as well as the risk of runs on both, provide a rationale for requiring stable NAV MMFs to reorganize as special purpose banks (SPBs) subject to banking oversight and regulation. As banks, MMFs could have access to government insurance and lender-of-last-resort facilities. An advantage of such a reorganization could be that it uses a well-understood regulatory framework for the mitigation of systemic risk. But while the conceptual basis for this option is fairly straightforward, its implementation might take a broad range of forms and would probably require legislation together with interagency coordination. An important hurdle for successful conversion of MMFs to SPBs may be the very large amounts of equity necessary to capitalize the new banks. In addition, to the extent that deposits in the new SPBs would be insured, the potential government liabilities through deposit insurance would be increased substantially, and the development of an appropriate pricing scheme for such insurance would present some of the same challenges as the pricing of deposit insurance. More broadly, the possible interactions between the new SPBs and the existing banking system would have to be studied carefully by policymakers.

(h) Enhanced constraints on unregulated MMF substitutes. New measures intended to mitigate MMF risks may also reduce the appeal of MMFs to many investors. While it is likely that some (particularly retail) investors may move their assets from MMFs to bank deposits if regulation of MMFs becomes too burdensome and meaningfully reduces MMF returns, others may be motivated to shift assets to unregulated funds with stable NAVs, such as offshore MMFs, enhanced cash funds, and other stable value vehicles. Such funds, which typically hold assets similar to those held by MMFs, are vulnerable to runs but are less transparent and less constrained than MMFs, so their growth would likely pose systemic risks. Hence, effective mitigation of this risk may require policy reforms targeting regulatory arbitrage. Reforms of this type generally would require legislation and action by the SEC and other agencies.

1. **Introduction and Background**

   a. Money Market Funds

   MMFs are mutual funds that offer individuals, businesses, and governments a convenient and cost-effective means of pooled investing in money market instruments. MMFs provide an economically important service by acting as intermediaries between shareholders who desire liquid investments, often for cash management, and borrowers who seek term funding.

   With nearly $3 trillion in assets under management, MMFs are important providers of credit to businesses, financial institutions, and governments. Indeed, these funds play a dominant role in some short-term credit markets. For example, MMFs own almost 40 percent of outstanding commercial paper, roughly two-thirds of short-term state and local government debt, and significant portions of outstanding short-term Treasury and federal agency securities.

   Like other mutual funds, MMFs are regulated under the Investment Company Act of 1940 (ICA). In addition to the requirements applicable to other funds under the ICA, MMFs must comply with rule 2a-7, which permits these funds to maintain a "stable" net asset value (NAV) per share, typically $1, through the use of the "amortized cost" method of valuation. Under this method, securities are valued at acquisition cost, with adjustments for amortization of premium or accretion of discount, instead of at fair market value. To prevent substantial deviations between the $1 share price and the mark-to-market per-share value of the fund's assets (its "shadow NAV"), a MMF must periodically compare the two. If there is a difference of more than one-half of 1 percent (or $0.005 per share), the fund must re-price its shares, an event colloquially known as "breaking the buck."

   Historically, the stable NAV has played an important role in distinguishing MMFs from other mutual funds and in facilitating the use of MMFs as cash management vehicles. Rule 2a-7 also imposes credit-quality, maturity, and diversification requirements on MMF portfolios designed to ensure that the funds' investing remains consistent with the objective of maintaining a stable NAV. A MMF's $1 share price is not guaranteed through any form of deposit or other insurance, or otherwise—indeed, MMF prospectuses must state that shares can lose value. However, by permitting amortized cost valuation, rule 2a-7 affords MMFs price stability under normal market conditions.

   MMFs pursue a range of investment objectives, with corresponding differences in portfolio composition. For example, tax-exempt MMFs purchase short-term municipal securities and offer tax-exempt income to fund shareholders, while Treasury-only MMFs hold only obligations of the U.S. Treasury. In contrast, prime MMFs invest largely in private debt instruments, such as commercial paper and certificates of deposit, and, commensurate with the greater risks in prime MMF portfolios, they generally pay higher yields than Treasury-only funds.

MMFs are marketed both to retail investors (that is, individuals), for whom MMFs are the only means of investing in many money market instruments, and to institutions, which are often attracted by the convenience and cost efficiency of MMFs, even though many institutional investors have the ability to invest directly in the instruments held by MMFs. Institutional MMFs, which currently account for about two-thirds of the assets under management in MMFs, have grown much faster, on net, in the past two decades than retail funds. The rapid growth of institutional funds has important implications for the MMF industry, because institutional funds tend to have more volatile flows and more yield-sensitive shareholders than retail funds.

MMFs compete with other stable-value, low-risk investments. Because MMFs generally maintain stable NAVs, offer redemptions on demand, and often provide services that compete with those offered to holders of insured deposits (such as transactions services), many retail customers likely consider MMF shares and bank deposits as near substitutes, even if the two classes of products are fundamentally different (most notably because MMF shares are not insured and because MMFs and banks are subject to very different regulatory regimes). Some institutional investors may also view bank deposits and MMFs as near substitutes, although usual limitations on deposit insurance coverage and interest payments on deposits likely reduce the attractiveness of bank deposits for most such investors.[2] Institutional investors also have access to less-regulated MMF substitutes (for example, offshore MMFs, enhanced cash funds, and other stable value vehicles) and may perceive them as near substitutes for MMFs, even if those vehicles are not subject to the protections afforded by rule 2a-7.

b. *MMFs' Susceptibility to Runs*

In the twenty-seven years since the adoption of rule 2a-7, only two MMFs have broken the buck. In 1994, a small MMF suffered a capital loss because of exposures to interest rate derivatives, but the event passed without significant repercussions. In contrast, as further discussed later, when the Reserve Primary Fund broke the buck in September 2008, it helped ignite a massive run on prime MMFs that contributed to severe dislocations in short-term credit markets and strains on the businesses and institutions that obtain funding in those markets.[3]

Although the run on MMFs in 2008 is itself unique in the history of the industry, the events of 2008 underscored the susceptibility of MMFs to runs. That susceptibility arises because, when shareholders perceive a risk that a fund will suffer losses, each

---

[2] Under the Federal Deposit Insurance Corporation's (FDIC) Temporary Liquidity Guarantee Program, coverage limits on noninterest-bearing transaction deposits in FDIC-insured institutions were temporarily lifted beginning in October 2008 and coverage will extend through 2010. Effective December 31, 2010, pursuant to the Dodd-Frank Wall Street Reform and Consumer Protection Act, P.L. 111-203, ("Dodd-Frank Act"), all noninterest-bearing transaction deposits will have unlimited coverage until January 1, 2013. In addition, section 627 of the Dodd-Frank Act repeals the prohibition on banks paying interest on corporate demand deposit accounts effective July 21, 2011.

[3] Section 1(c) contains more detail on the MMF industry's experience during the recent financial crisis.

shareholder has an incentive to redeem shares before other shareholders. Five features of MMFs, their sponsors, and their investors principally contribute to this incentive:

(i) Maturity transformation with limited liquidity resources. One important economic function of MMFs is their role as intermediaries between shareholders who want liquid investments and borrowers who desire term funding. As such, MMFs offer shares that are payable on demand, but they invest both in cash-like instruments and in short-term securities that are less liquid, including, for example, term commercial paper. Redemptions in excess of MMFs' cash-like liquidity may force funds to sell less liquid assets. When money markets are strained, funds may not be able to obtain full value (that is, amortized cost) for such assets in secondary markets and may incur losses as a consequence. Investors thus have an incentive to redeem shares *before* a fund has depleted its cash-like instruments (which serve as its liquidity buffer).

(ii) NAVs rounded to $1. Share prices of MMFs are rounded to the nearest cent, typically resulting in a $1 NAV per share. The rounding fosters an expectation that MMF share prices will not fluctuate, which exacerbates investors' incentive to run when there is risk that prices *will* fluctuate. When a MMF that has experienced a small (less than one-half of 1 percent) capital loss redeems shares at the full $1 NAV, it concentrates the loss among the remaining shareholders. Thus, redemptions from such a fund further depress the market value of its assets per share outstanding (its shadow NAV), and redemptions of sufficient scale may cause the fund to break the buck. Early redeemers are therefore more likely to receive the usual $1 NAV than those who wait.

(iii) Portfolios exposed to credit and interest rate risks. MMFs invest in securities with credit and interest-rate risks. Although these risks are generally small given the short maturity of the securities and the high degree of portfolio diversification, even a small capital loss, in combination with other features of MMFs, can trigger a significant volume of redemptions. The events of September 2008—when losses on Lehman Brothers Holdings, Inc. (Lehman Brothers) debt instruments caused just one MMF to break the buck and triggered a broad run on MMFs—highlight the fact that credit losses at even a single fund may have serious implications for the whole industry and consequently for the entire financial system.[4]

(iv) Discretionary sponsor capital support. MMFs invest in assets that may lose value, but the funds have no formal capital buffers or insurance to maintain their $1 share prices in the event of a loss on a portfolio asset.

The MMF industry's record of maintaining a stable NAV reflects, in part, substantial discretionary intervention by MMF sponsors (that is, fund advisers, their affiliates, and their parent firms) to support funds that otherwise might have broken the

---

[4] Souring credits and rapid increases in interest rates have adversely affected MMFs on other occasions. For example, beginning in the summer of 2007, MMF exposures to structured investment vehicles and other asset-backed commercial paper caused capital losses at many MMFs, and many MMF sponsors voluntarily provided capital support that prevented some funds from breaking the buck.

buck.[5] Sponsors do not commit to support an MMF in advance, because an explicit commitment may require the sponsor to consolidate the fund on its balance sheet and—if the sponsor is subject to regulatory capital requirements—hold additional regulatory capital against the contingent exposure. Nor is there any requirement that sponsors support ailing MMFs; such a mandate would transform the nature of MMF shares by shifting risks from investors to sponsors and probably would require government supervision and monitoring of sponsors' resources and capital adequacy.[6] Instead, sponsor capital support remains expressly voluntary, and not all MMFs have a sponsor capable of fully supporting its MMFs. Nonetheless, a long history of such support probably has contributed substantially to the perceived safety of MMFs.

However, the possibility that sponsors may become unwilling or unable to provide expected support during a crisis is itself a source of systemic risk. Indeed, sponsor support is probably least reliable when systemic risks are most salient.[7] Moreover, MMFs without deep-pocketed sponsors remain vulnerable to runs that can affect the entire industry. The Reserve Primary Fund was not the only MMF that held Lehman Brothers debt at the time of the Lehman Brothers' bankruptcy in September 2008, but it broke the buck because the Reserve Primary Fund, unlike some of its competitors, had substantial holdings of Lehman Brothers debt and Reserve did not have the resources to support its fund. Investors also recognized the riskiness of sponsor support more broadly during the run on MMFs in 2008. For example, outflows from prime MMFs following the Lehman Brothers bankruptcy tended to be larger among MMFs with sponsors that were themselves under strain (as measured by credit default swap spreads for parent firms or affiliates), indicating that MMF investors quickly redeemed shares on concerns about sponsors' potential inabilities to bolster ailing funds.

(v) Investors' low risk tolerance and expectations. Investors have come to view MMF shares as extremely safe, in part because of the funds' stable NAVs and sponsors' record of supporting funds that might otherwise lose value. MMFs' history of maintaining stable value has attracted highly risk-averse investors who are prone to withdraw assets rapidly when losses appear possible.

MMFs, like other mutual funds, commit to redeem shares based on the fund's NAV at the time of redemption. MMFs are under no legal or regulatory requirement to redeem shares at $1; rule 2a-7 only requires that MMFs be managed to maintain a stable

---

[5] For example, more than 100 MMFs received sponsor capital support in 2007 and 2008 because of investments in securities that lost value and because of the run on MMFs in September and October 2008. See Securities and Exchange Commission (2009) "Money Market Reform: Proposed Rule," pp. 13-14, 17, and notes 38 and 54.

[6] Even discretionary support for MMFs may lead to concerns about the safety and soundness of MMF sponsors. Sponsors that foster expectations of such support may be granting a form of implicit recourse that is not reflected on sponsors' balance sheets or in their regulatory capital ratios, and such implicit recourse may contribute to broader systemic risk.

[7] Other forms of discretionary financial support, such as that provided by dealers for auction rate securities, did not fare well during the financial crisis.

NAV. Yet sponsor-supported stable, rounded NAVs and the typical $1 MMF share price foster investors' impressions that MMFs are extremely safe investments. Indeed, the growth of retail MMFs in recent decades may have reflected some substitution from insured deposits at commercial banks, thrifts, and credit unions, particularly as MMFs have offered transactions services and other bank-like functions. Although MMF shares, unlike bank deposits, are not government insured and are not backed by capital to absorb losses, this distinction may have become even less clear to retail investors following the unprecedented government support of MMFs in 2008 and 2009. Furthermore, that recent support may have left even sophisticated institutional investors with the mistaken impression that MMF safety is enhanced because the government stands ready to support the industry again with the same tools employed at the height of the financial crisis.

The growth of institutional MMFs in recent years probably has heightened both the risk aversion of the typical MMF shareholder and the volatility of MMF cash flows. Many institutional investors cannot tolerate fluctuations in share prices for a variety of reasons. In addition, institutional investors are typically more sophisticated than retail investors in obtaining and analyzing information about MMF portfolios and risks, have larger amounts at stake, and hence are quicker to respond to events that may threaten the stable NAV. In fact, institutional MMFs have historically experienced much more volatile flows than retail funds. During the run on MMFs in September 2008, institutional funds accounted for more than 90 percent of the net redemptions from prime MMFs.

The interaction of these five features is critical. Taken alone, each of the features just listed probably would only modestly increase the vulnerability of MMFs to runs, but, in combination, the features tend to amplify and reinforce one another. For example, equity mutual funds perform maturity transformation and take on capital risks, but even after large capital losses, outflows from equity funds tend to be small relative to assets, most likely because equity funds are not marketed for their ability to maintain stable NAVs, do not attract the risk-averse investor base that characterizes MMFs, and offer the opportunity for capital appreciation. If MMFs with rounded NAVs had lacked sponsor support over the past few decades, many might have broken the buck and diminished the expectation of a stable $1 share price. In that case, investors who nonetheless elected to hold shares in such funds might have become more tolerant of risk and less inclined to run. If MMFs had attracted primarily a retail investor base rather than an institutional base, investors might be slower to respond to strains on a MMF. And even a highly risk-averse investor base would not necessarily make MMFs susceptible to runs—and to contagion arising from runs on other MMFs—if funds had a credible means to guarantee their $1 NAVs. Thus, policy responses that diminish the reinforcing interactions among the features discussed herein hold promise for muting overall risks posed by MMFs.

c. *MMFs in the Recent Financial Crisis*

The turmoil in financial markets in 2007 and 2008 caused severe strains both among MMFs and in the short-term debt markets in which MMFs invest. Beginning in mid-2007, dozens of funds faced losses from holdings of highly rated asset-backed commercial paper (ABCP) issued by structured investment vehicles (SIVs), some of which had exposures to the subprime mortgage market. Fear of such losses at one MMF caused that fund to experience a substantial run in August 2007, which was brought under control when the fund's sponsor purchased more than $5 billion of illiquid securities from the fund. Indeed, financial support from MMF sponsors in recent years probably prevented a number of funds from breaking the buck because of losses on SIV paper.

The crisis for MMFs worsened considerably in September 2008 with the bankruptcy of Lehman Brothers on September 15 and mounting concerns about other issuers of commercial paper, particularly financial firms. The Reserve Primary Fund, a $62 billion MMF, held $785 million in Lehman Brothers debt on the day of Lehman Brothers' bankruptcy and immediately began experiencing a run—shareholders requested redemptions of approximately $40 billion in just two days. In order to meet the redemptions, the Reserve Primary Fund depleted its cash reserves and began seeking to sell its portfolio securities, which further depressed their valuations. Unlike other MMFs that held distressed securities, the Reserve Primary Fund had no affiliate with sufficient resources to support its $1 NAV, and Reserve announced on September 16 that its Primary Fund would break the buck and re-price its shares at $0.97. On September 22, the SEC issued an order permitting the suspension of redemptions in certain Reserve MMFs to permit their orderly liquidation.

The run quickly spread to other prime MMFs, which held sizable amounts of financial sector debt that investors feared might decline rapidly in value. During the week of September 15, 2008, investors withdrew approximately $310 billion (15 percent of assets) from prime MMFs, with the heaviest redemptions coming from institutional funds. To meet these redemption requests, MMFs depleted their cash positions and sought to sell portfolio securities into already illiquid markets. These efforts caused further declines in the prices of short-term instruments and put pressure on per-share values of fund portfolios, threatening MMFs' stable NAVs. Nonetheless, only one MMF—the Reserve Primary Fund—broke the buck, because many MMF sponsors provided substantial financial support to prevent capital losses in their funds.

Fearing further redemptions, many MMF advisers limited new portfolio investments to cash, U.S. Treasury securities, and overnight instruments, and avoided term commercial paper, certificates of deposit, and other short-term credit instruments. During September 2008, MMFs reduced their holdings of commercial paper by about $170 billion (25 percent). As market participants hoarded cash and refused to lend to one another on more than an overnight basis, interest rates spiked and short-term credit markets froze. Commercial paper issuers were required to make significant draws on their backup lines of credit, placing additional pressure on the balance sheets of commercial banks.

On September 19, 2008, Treasury and the Board of Governors of the Federal Reserve System (Federal Reserve) announced two unprecedented market interventions to stabilize MMFs and to provide liquidity to short-term funding markets. Treasury's Temporary Guarantee Program for Money Market Funds temporarily provided guarantees for shareholders in MMFs that elected to participate in the program.[8] The Federal Reserve's Asset-Backed Commercial Paper Money Market Mutual Fund Liquidity Facility (AMLF) extended credit to U.S. banks and bank holding companies to finance their purchases of high-quality ABCP from MMFs.[9]

The announcements of these government programs substantially slowed the run on prime MMFs. Outflows from prime MMFs diminished to about $65 billion in the week after the announcements and, by mid-October, these MMFs began attracting net inflows. Moreover, in the weeks following the government interventions, markets for commercial paper and other short-term debt instruments stabilized considerably.[10]

2. The SEC's Changes to the Regulation of MMFs

The effects of the financial turmoil in 2007 and 2008 on MMFs—and, in particular, the run on these funds in September 2008 and its consequences—have highlighted the need for reforms to mitigate the systemic risks posed by MMFs. Appropriate reforms include changes to MMF regulations as well as broader policy actions. This section first examines rule changes that have been adopted by the SEC to improve the safety and resilience of MMFs and then discusses some limitations in these measures' mitigation of systemic risk and the need for further reforms.

Notwithstanding the need for reform, the significance of MMFs in the U.S. financial system suggests that changes must be considered carefully. Tighter restrictions on MMFs might, for example, lead to a reduction in the supply of short-term credit, a shift in assets to substitute investment vehicles that are subject to less regulation than MMFs, and significant impairment of an important cash-management tool for investors. Moreover, the economic importance of risk-taking by MMFs—as lenders in private debt markets and as investments that appeal to shareholders' preferences for risk and return—suggests that the appropriate objective for reform should not be to eliminate all risks posed by MMFs. Attempting to prevent any fund from *ever* breaking the buck would be an impractical goal that might lead, for example, to draconian and—from a broad

---

[8] MMFs that elected to participate in the program paid fees of 4 to 6 basis points at an annual rate for the guarantee. The Temporary Guarantee Program for Money Market Funds expired on September 18, 2009.

[9] The AMLF expired on February 1, 2010.

[10] Several other unprecedented government interventions that provided additional support for the MMF industry and for short-term funding markets were introduced after the run on MMFs had largely abated. For example, the Federal Reserve in October 2008 established the Commercial Paper Funding Facility (CPFF), which provided loans for purchases (through a special purpose vehicle) of term commercial paper from issuers. The CPFF, which expired on February 1, 2010, helped issuers repay investors—such as MMFs—who held maturing paper. Also in October 2008, the Federal Reserve announced the Money Market Investor Funding Facility (MMIFF), which was intended to bolster liquidity for MMFs by financing (through special purpose vehicles) purchases of securities from the funds. The MMIFF was never used and expired on October 30, 2009. In November 2008, Treasury agreed to become a buyer of last resort for certain securities held by the Reserve U.S. Government Fund (a MMF), in order to facilitate an orderly and timely liquidation of the fund. Under the agreement, Treasury would purchase certain securities issued by government sponsored enterprises at amortized cost (not mark to market), and $3.6 billion of such purchases were completed in January 2009.

economic perspective—counterproductive measures, such as outright prohibitions on purchases of private debt instruments and securities with maturities of more than one day. Instead, policymakers should balance the benefits of allowing individual MMFs to take some risks and facilitating private and public borrowers' access to term financing in money markets with the broader objective of mitigating systemic risks—in particular, the risk that one fund's problems may cause serious harm to other MMFs, their shareholders, short-term funding markets, the financial system, and the economy.

a. SEC Regulatory Changes

In January 2010, the SEC adopted new rules regulating MMFs in order to make these funds more resilient to market disruptions and thus less likely to break the buck. The new rules also might help reduce the likelihood of runs on MMFs by facilitating the orderly liquidation of funds that have broken the buck. The SEC designed the new rules primarily to meet its statutory obligations under the ICA to protect investors and promote capital formation. Nonetheless, the rules should mitigate (although not eliminate) systemic risks by reducing the susceptibility of MMFs to runs, both by lessening the likelihood that an individual fund will break the buck and by containing the damage should one break the buck. The rule changes fall into three principal categories.

(i) Enhanced Risk-Limiting Constraints on Money Market Fund Portfolios. Each of the changes that follow further constrain risk-taking by MMFs.

Liquidity Risk. One of the most important SEC rule changes aimed at reducing systemic risk associated with MMFs is a requirement that each fund maintain a substantial liquidity cushion. Augmented liquidity should position MMFs to better withstand heavy redemptions without selling portfolio securities into potentially distressed markets at discounted prices. Forced "fire sales" to meet heavy redemptions may cause losses not only for the fund that must sell the securities, but also for other MMFs that hold the same or similar securities. Thus, a substantial liquidity cushion should help reduce the risk that strains on one MMF will be transmitted to other funds and to short-term credit markets.

Specifically, the SEC's new rules require that MMFs maintain minimum daily and weekly liquidity positions. Daily liquidity, which must be at least 10 percent of a MMF's assets, includes cash, U.S. Treasury obligations, and securities (including repurchase agreements) that mature or for which the fund has a contractual right to obtain cash within a day. Weekly liquidity, which must be at least 30 percent of each MMF's assets, includes cash, securities that mature or can be converted to cash within a week, U.S. Treasury obligations, and securities issued by federal government agencies and government-sponsored enterprises with remaining maturities of 60 days or less.[11]

---

[11] Tax-exempt money market funds are exempt from daily minimum liquidity requirements but not the weekly minimum liquidity requirements, because most tax-exempt fund portfolios consist of longer-term floating- and variable-rate securities with seven-day "put" options that effectively give the funds weekly liquidity. Tax-exempt funds are unlikely to have investment alternatives that would permit them to meet a daily liquidity requirement.

Furthermore, the new rules require MMF advisers to maintain larger liquidity buffers as necessary to meet reasonably foreseeable redemptions.

Credit Risk. The new rules reduce MMFs' maximum allowable holdings of "second-tier" securities, which carry more credit risk than first-tier securities, to no more than 3 percent of each fund's assets.[12] In addition, a MMF's exposure to a single second-tier issuer is now limited to one-half of 1 percent of the fund's assets, and funds can only purchase second-tier securities with maturities of 45 days or less. These new constraints reduce the likelihood that individual funds will be exposed to a credit event that could cause the funds to break the buck. Also, since second-tier securities often trade in thinner markets, these changes should improve the ability of individual MMFs to maintain a stable NAV during periods of market volatility.

Interest Rate Risk. By reducing the maximum allowable weighted average maturity (WAM) of fund portfolios from 90 days to 60 days, the new rules are intended to diminish funds' exposure to interest rate risk and increase the liquidity of fund portfolios. The SEC also introduced a new weighted average life (WAL) measure for MMFs—and set a ceiling for WAL at 120 days—in order to lower funds' exposure to interest-rate, credit, and liquidity risks associated with the floating-rate obligations that MMFs commonly hold.[13]

Stress Testing. Finally, the SEC's new rules require fund advisers to periodically stress test their funds' ability to maintain a stable NAV per share based on certain hypothetical events, including a change in short-term interest rates, an increase in shareholder redemptions, a downgrade or default of a portfolio security, and a change in interest rate spreads. Regular and methodical monitoring of these risks and their potential effects should help funds weather stress without incident.

(ii) Facilitating Orderly Fund Liquidations. The new SEC rules should reduce the systemic risk posed by MMFs by permitting a fund that is breaking the buck to promptly suspend redemptions and liquidate its portfolio in an orderly manner. This new rule should help prevent a capital loss at one fund from forcing a disorderly sale of portfolio securities that might disrupt short-term markets and diminish share values of other MMFs. Moreover, the ability of a fund to suspend redemptions should help prevent investors who redeem shares from benefiting at the expense of those who remain invested in a fund.

---

[12] Under SEC rule 2a-7, for short-term debt securities to qualify as second-tier securities, they generally must have received the second highest short-term debt rating from the credit rating agencies or be of comparable quality. Section 939A of the Dodd-Frank Act requires that government agencies remove references to credit ratings in their rules and replace them with other credit standards that the agency determines appropriate. As a result, the SEC will be reconsidering this rule and its provisions relating to second-tier securities to comply with this statutory mandate.

[13] For purposes of computing WAM, a floating-rate security's "maturity" can be its next interest-rate reset date. In computing WAL, the life of a security is determined solely by its final maturity date. Hence, WAL should be more useful than WAM in reflecting the risks of widening spreads on longer-term floating-rate securities.

(iii) Repurchase Agreements. The SEC's new rules place more stringent constraints on repurchase agreements that are collateralized with private debt instruments rather than cash equivalents or government securities. MMFs are among the largest purchasers of repurchase agreements, which they use to invest cash, typically on an overnight basis. Because the collateral usually consists of long-term debt securities, a MMF cannot hold the securities underlying this collateral without violating SEC rules that limit MMF holdings to short-term obligations. Accordingly, if a significant counterparty fails to repurchase securities as stipulated in a repurchase agreement, its MMF counterparties can be expected to direct custodians to sell the collateral immediately, and sales of private debt instruments could be sizable and disruptive to financial markets. To address this risk, the SEC's new rule places additional constraints on MMFs' exposure to counterparties through repurchase agreement transactions that are collateralized by securities other than cash equivalents or government securities.

b. *Need for Further Reform to Reduce Susceptibility to Runs*

The new SEC rules make MMFs more resilient and less risky and therefore reduce the likelihood of runs on funds, increase the size of runs that they could withstand, and mitigate the systemic risks they pose. However, more can be done to address the structural vulnerabilities of MMFs to runs. Indeed, the Chairman of the SEC characterized its new rules as "a first step" in strengthening MMFs and noted that a number of additional possible reforms (many of which are presented in section 3 of this report) are under discussion. Likewise, Treasury's *Financial Regulatory Reform: A New Foundation* (2009) anticipated that measures taken by the SEC "should not, by themselves, be expected to prevent a run on MMFs of the scale experienced in September 2008."

Of the five features that make MMFs vulnerable to runs (see section 1(b)), the two most directly addressed in the new SEC rules are liquidity risks associated with maturity transformation and MMF portfolios' exposures to credit and interest-rate risks. The SEC's new rules should substantially reduce these risks, but systemic risks arising from the other features of MMFs and their investors—the stable, rounded NAV, a system of discretionary sponsor support, and a highly risk-averse investor base—still remain, as do many of the amplifying interaction effects. Some mitigation of the destabilizing effects that one or a few MMFs can impose on the rest of the industry through contagion might be achievable through further modifications to rule 2a-7 and other SEC rules. Importantly, however, other reforms that could more substantially reduce the risk of contagion and that, as such, merit further consideration, would require action beyond what the SEC could achieve under its current authority.

Mitigating the risk of runs before another liquidity crisis materializes is especially important because the events of September 2008 may have induced expectations of government assistance at minimal cost in case of severe financial strains. Market participants know, and recent events have confirmed, that when runs on MMFs occur, the government will face substantial pressure to intervene in some manner to minimize the propagation of financial strains to short-term funding markets and to the real economy. Importantly, such interventions would be intended not only to reduce harm to MMF investors but also to prevent disruptions of markets for commercial paper and other short-term financing instruments, which are critical for the functioning of the economy. Therefore, if further measures to insulate the industry from systemic risk are not taken *before* the next liquidity crisis, market participants will likely expect that the government would provide emergency support at minimal cost for MMFs *during* the next crisis. Such market expectations of (hypothetical) future non-priced or subsidized government support would distort incentives for MMFs and prices in short-term funding markets and would potentially increase the systemic risk posed by MMFs. To forestall these perverse effects, it is thus imperative that MMFs be required to internalize fully the costs of liquidity or other risks associated with their operation.

MMF regulatory reform in light of the run on MMFs in September and October 2008. The run on MMFs in 2008 provides some important lessons for evaluating potential reforms for mitigating systemic risk. For example, the triggering events of the run and the magnitude of the outflows that followed underscore the difficulty of designing reforms that might prevent runs and the associated damage to the financial system.

Making each individual MMF robust enough to survive a crisis of the size of that experienced in 2008 may not be an appropriate policy objective because it would unduly limit risk taking. Indeed, although the SEC's tightening of restrictions on the liquidity, interest-rate, and credit risks borne by individual MMFs will be helpful in making MMFs more resilient to future strains, there are practical limits to the degree of systemic risk mitigation that can be achieved through further restrictions of this type. For example, an objective of preventing any MMF from breaking the buck probably would not be feasible for funds that invest in private debt markets. Changes that would prevent funds from breaking the buck due to a single Lehman Brothers-like exposure would have to be severe: Only limiting funds' exposures to each issuer to less than one-half of 1 percent of assets would prevent a precipitous drop in the value of any single issuer's debt from causing a MMF to break the buck.[14] But even such a limit on exposure to a single issuer would not address the risk that MMFs may accumulate exposures to distinct but highly correlated issuers, and that funds would remain vulnerable to events that cause the debt of multiple issuers to lose value.

Beyond diversification limits, new rules to protect MMFs from material credit losses would be difficult to craft unless regulators take the extreme step of eliminating funds' ability to hold *any* risky assets. But that approach would be clearly undesirable, as it would adversely affect many firms that obtain short-term financing through commercial paper and similar instruments. In addition, such an extreme approach would deny many retail investors any opportunity to obtain exposure to private money market instruments and most likely would motivate some institutional investors to shift assets from MMFs to less regulated vehicles.

---

[14] At the time of its bankruptcy, Lehman Brothers' short-term debt was still a first-tier security, so MMFs were able to hold up to 5 percent of their assets in Lehman Brothers' debt. The SEC's new rules do not affect this limit.

Similarly, liquidity requirements sufficient to cover all redemption scenarios for MMFs probably would be impractical and inefficient. The SEC's new liquidity requirements help mitigate liquidity risks borne by the funds, and if MMFs had held enough liquid assets in September 2008 to meet the new liquidity requirements, each MMF would have had adequate daily liquidity to meet redemption requests on most individual days during the run. Even so, the cumulative effect of severe outflows on *consecutive* days would have exceeded many funds' liquidity buffers. Moreover, without external support in 2008—specifically, the introduction of the Treasury's Temporary Guarantee Program for Money Market Funds and the Federal Reserve's AMLF— outflows likely would have continued and been much larger, and they would have forced substantial sales of assets to meet redemptions. Such asset sales would have contributed to severe strains in short-term markets, depressed asset prices, caused capital losses for MMFs, and prompted further shareholder flight. Hence, MMFs' experience during the run in 2008 indicates that the new SEC liquidity requirements make individual MMFs more resilient to shocks but still leave them susceptible to runs of substantial scale.

Raising the liquidity requirements enough so that each MMF would hold adequate daily liquidity to withstand a large-scale run would be a severe constraint and would fail to take advantage of risk-pooling opportunities that might be exploited by external sources of liquidity. During the run in 2008, individual MMFs experienced large variations in the timing and magnitude of their redemptions. Liquidity requirements stringent enough to ensure that every individual MMF could have met redemptions without selling assets would have left most of the industry with far too much liquidity, even during the run, and would have created additional liquidity risks for issuers of short-term securities, since these issuers would have had to roll over paper more frequently. Some of the approaches discussed in section 3 are aimed at buttressing the SEC's new minimum liquidity requirements without simply increasing their magnitude.

Finally, the run on MMFs in 2008 demonstrated the systemic threat that such runs may represent. Without additional reforms to more fully mitigate the risk of a run spreading among MMFs, the actions to support the MMF industry that the U.S. government took beginning in 2008 may create an expectation for similar government support during future financial crises, and the resulting moral hazard may make crises in the MMF industry more frequent than the historical record would suggest. Accordingly, despite the risk reduction that should be achieved by the initial set of new SEC rules, policymakers should explore the advantages and disadvantages of implementing further reforms before another crisis materializes.

3. Policy Options for Further Reducing the Risks of Runs on MMFs

This section discusses a range of options for further mitigation of the systemic risks posed by MMFs. The SEC requested comment on some of these options, such as requiring that MMFs maintain a floating NAV or requiring in kind redemptions in certain circumstances. In addition, the SEC received comments proposing a two-tier system of MMFs in which some funds maintain a stable NAV and others a floating NAV. Other options discussed in this section go beyond what the SEC could implement under existing authorities and would require legislation or coordinated action by multiple government agencies and the MMF industry. While the measures presented here, either individually or in combination, would help diminish systemic risk, new restrictions imposed solely on MMFs may reduce their appeal to some investors and might cause some—primarily institutional—investors to move assets to less regulated cash management substitutes. Many such funds, like MMFs, seek to maintain a stable NAV and have other features that make them vulnerable to runs, so such funds likely also would pose systemic risks. Therefore, effective mitigation of MMFs' susceptibility to runs may require policy reforms beyond those directed at registered MMFs to address risks posed by funds that compete with MMFs. Such reforms, which generally would require legislation, are discussed in section 3(h).

a. Floating Net Asset Values

Historically, the $1 stable NAV that MMFs maintain under rule 2a-7 has been a key element of their appeal to a broad range of investors, and the stable NAV has contributed to a dramatic expansion in MMFs' assets over the past two decades. At the same time, as noted in section 1(b), the stable, rounded NAV is one of the features that heighten the vulnerability of MMFs to runs. The significance of MMFs in financial markets and the central role of the stable, rounded NAV in making MMFs appealing to investors and, at the same time, vulnerable to runs, make careful discussion of the potential benefits and risks of moving MMFs away from a stable NAV essential to a discussion of MMF reform.

The stable, rounded NAVs of MMFs contribute to their vulnerability to runs for several reasons.

- First, the stable, rounded NAV, coupled with MMF sponsors' longstanding practice of supporting the stable NAV when funds have encountered difficulties, has fostered investors' expectations that MMF shares are risk-free cash equivalents. When the Reserve Primary Fund failed to maintain those expectations in September 2008, the sudden loss of investor confidence helped precipitate a generalized run on MMFs.

  By making gains and losses a regular occurrence, as they are in other mutual funds, a floating NAV could alter investor expectations and make clear that MMFs are not risk-free vehicles. Thus, investors might become more accustomed to and tolerant of NAV fluctuations and less prone to sudden, destabilizing reactions in the face of even modest losses. However, the substantial changes in investor expectations that could result from a floating NAV also might motivate investors to shift assets away from MMFs to banks or to unregulated cash-management vehicles, and the effects of potentially large movements of assets on the financial system should be considered carefully. These issues are discussed in more detail later.

- Second, a rounded NAV may accelerate runs by amplifying investors' incentives to redeem shares quickly if a fund is at risk of a capital loss. When a MMF experiences a loss of less than one-half of 1 percent and continues to redeem shares at a rounded NAV of $1, it offers redeeming shareholders an arbitrage opportunity by paying more for the shares than the shares are worth. Simultaneously, the fund drives down the expected future value of the shares because redemptions at $1 per share further erode the fund's market-based per-share value—and increase the likelihood that the fund will break the buck—as losses on portfolio assets are spread over a shrinking asset base. These dynamics are inherently unstable. Thus, even an investor who otherwise might not choose to redeem may do so in recognition of other shareholders' incentives to redeem and the effects of such redemptions on a fund's expected NAV. The growth of institutional investment in MMFs has exacerbated this instability because institutional investors are better positioned than retail investors to identify potential problems in a MMF's portfolio and rapidly withdraw significant amounts of assets from the fund.

In contrast, a floating NAV eliminates *some* of the incentives to redeem when a MMF has experienced a loss. Because MMFs must redeem shares at NAVs set *after* redemption requests are received, losses incurred by a fund with a floating NAV are borne on a pro rata basis by all shareholders, whether they redeem or not. Redemptions from such a fund do not concentrate already incurred losses over a smaller asset base and do not create clear arbitrage opportunities for investors. However, as discussed below, a floating NAV does not eliminate the incentive to redeem shares from a distressed MMF.

- Third, the SEC rules that permit funds to maintain a stable, rounded NAV also force an abrupt decrease in price once the difference between a fund's market-based shadow NAV and its $1 stable NAV exceeds one-half of 1 percent. So, although NAV fluctuations are rare in MMFs, when prices do decline, the change appears as a sudden drop. This discontinuity heightens investors' incentives to redeem shares before a loss is incurred, produces dire headlines, and probably raises the chance of a panic.

These considerations suggest that moving to a floating NAV would reduce the systemic risk posed by MMFs to some extent. Under a required floating NAV, MMFs would have to value their portfolio assets just like any other mutual fund. That is, MMFs would not be able to round their NAVs to $1 or use the accounting methods (for example, amortized cost for portfolio securities with a maturity of greater than 60 days) currently allowed under rule 2a-7.

To be sure, a floating NAV itself would not eliminate entirely MMFs' susceptibility to runs. Rational investors still would have an incentive to redeem as fast as possible the shares of any MMF that is at risk of depleting its liquidity buffer before that buffer is exhausted, because subsequent redemptions may force the fund to dispose of less-liquid assets and incur losses. However, investors would have less of an incentive to run from MMFs with floating NAVs than from those with stable, rounded NAVs.

Notwithstanding the advantages of a floating NAV, elimination of the stable NAV for MMFs would be a dramatic change for a nearly $3 trillion asset-management sector that has been built around the stable $1 share price. Indeed, a switch to floating NAVs for MMFs raises several concerns.

- First, such a change might reduce investor demand for MMFs and thus diminish their capacity to supply credit to businesses, financial institutions, state and local governments, and other borrowers who obtain financing in short-term debt markets. MMFs are the dominant providers of some types of credit, such as commercial paper and short-term municipal debt, so a significant contraction of MMFs might cause particular difficulties for borrowers who rely on these instruments for financing. If the contraction were abrupt, redemptions might cause severe disruptions for MMFs, the markets for the instruments the funds hold, and borrowers who tap those markets.

  While there is no direct evidence on the likely effect of a floating NAV on the demand for MMFs, the risk of a substantial shift of assets away from MMFs and into other vehicles should be weighed carefully. Assets under management in MMFs dwarf those of their nearest substitutes, such as, for example, ultra-short bond funds, most likely because ultra-short bond funds are not viewed as cash substitutes. To the extent that demand for stable NAV funds is boosted by investors who hold MMFs because they perceive them to be risk-free, a reduction in demand for these funds might be desirable.[15] However, some investors face functional obstacles to placing certain assets in floating NAV funds. For example, internal investment guidelines may prevent corporate cash managers from investing in floating NAV funds, some state laws allow municipalities to invest only in stable-value funds, and fiduciary obligations may prevent institutional investors from investing client money in floating NAV funds. In addition, some investors may not tolerate the loss of accounting convenience and tax efficiencies that would result from a shift to a floating NAV, although these problems might be mitigated somewhat through regulatory or legislative actions.[16]

- Second, a related concern is that elimination of MMFs' stable NAVs may cause investors to shift assets to stable NAV substitutes that are vulnerable to runs but subject to less regulation than MMFs. In particular, many institutional investors might move assets to less regulated or unregulated cash management vehicles, such as offshore MMFs, enhanced cash funds, and other stable value vehicles that hold portfolios similar to those of MMFs but are not subject to the ICA's restrictions on MMFs. These unregistered funds can take on more risks than MMFs, but such risks are not necessarily transparent to investors. Accordingly, unregistered funds may pose even greater systemic risks than MMFs, particularly if new restrictions on MMFs prompt substantial growth in unregistered funds. Thus, changes to MMF rules might displace or even increase systemic risks, rather than mitigate them, and make

---

[15] Even a contraction in the credit extended by MMFs might be an efficient outcome if such credit has been over-supplied because markets have not priced liquidity and systemic risks appropriately.

[16] A stable NAV relieves shareholders of the administrative task of tracking the timing and price of purchase and sale transactions for tax and accounting purposes. For investors using MMFs for cash management, floating NAV funds (under current rules) would present more record-keeping requirements than stable NAV funds, although certain tax changes beginning in 2011 will require mutual funds, including MMFs, to report the tax basis (presumably using an average basis method) to shareholders and thereby help reduce any associated accounting burden from a floating NAV.

such risks more difficult to monitor and control. Reforms designed to reduce risks in less regulated or unregulated MMF substitutes are discussed in more detail in section 3(h).

Elimination of MMFs' stable NAVs may also prompt some investors—particularly retail investors—to shift assets from MMFs to banks. Such asset shifts would have potential benefits and drawbacks, which are discussed in some detail in section 3(g).

- Third, MMFs' transition from stable to floating NAVs might itself be systemically risky. For example, if shareholders perceive a risk that a fund that is maintaining a $1 NAV under current rules has a market-based shadow NAV of less than $1, these investors may redeem shares preemptively to avoid potential losses when MMFs switch to floating NAVs. Shareholders who cannot tolerate floating NAVs probably also would redeem in advance. If large enough, redemptions could force some funds to sell assets and make concerns about losses self-fulfilling. Hence, successful implementation of a switch to floating NAVs would depend on careful design of the conversion process to guard against destabilizing transition dynamics.

- Fourth, risk management practices in a floating NAV MMF industry might deteriorate without the discipline required to maintain a $1 share price. MMFs comply with rule 2a-7 because doing so gives them the ability to use amortized-cost accounting to maintain a stable NAV. Without this reward, the incentive to follow 2a-7 restrictions is less clear. Moreover, the stable, rounded NAV creates a bright line for fund advisers: Losses in excess of ½ of 1 percent would be catastrophic because they would cause a fund to break the buck. With a floating NAV, funds would not have as clear a tipping point, so fund advisers might face reduced incentives for prudent risk management.

- The fifth and final concern is that a floating NAV that accomplishes its proponents' objectives of reducing systemic risks may be difficult to implement. Under normal market conditions, even a floating NAV would likely move very little because of the nature of MMF assets. For example, although a requirement that MMFs move to a $10 NAV and round to the nearest cent would force funds to reprice shares for as little as a 5 basis point change in portfolio value, NAV fluctuations might still remain relatively rare. Enhanced precision for NAVs (for example, NAVs with five significant figures) could bring more regular, incremental fluctuations, but precise pricing of many money market securities is challenging given the absence of active secondary markets. In addition, if fund sponsors decided to provide support to offset any small deviations from the usual NAV, deviations from that NAV might remain rare.

Thus, a floating NAV may not substantially improve investors' understanding of the riskiness of MMFs or reduce the stigma and systemic risks associated with breaking the buck. Investors' perceptions that MMFs are virtually riskless may change slowly and unpredictably if NAV fluctuations remain small and rare. MMFs with floating NAVs, at least temporarily, might even be more prone to runs if investors who continue to see shares as essentially risk-free react to small or temporary changes in the value of their shares.

To summarize, requiring the entire MMF industry to move to a floating NAV would have some potential benefits, but those benefits would have to be weighed carefully against the risks that such a change would entail.

b. *Private Emergency Liquidity Facilities for MMFs*

As discussed in section 1(b), the liquidity risk of MMFs contributes importantly to MMFs' vulnerability to runs. The programs introduced at the height of the run on MMFs in September 2008—Treasury's Temporary Guarantee Program for Money Market Funds and the liquidity backstop provided by the AMLF—were effective in stopping the run on MMFs.[17] More generally, policymakers have long recognized the utility of liquidity backstops for institutions engaged in maturity transformation: Banks, for example, have had access to the discount window since its inception, and backstop lending facilities also have been created more recently for other types of institutions. Thus, enhanced liquidity protection should be considered as part of any regulatory reform effort aimed at preventing runs on MMFs. At the same time, such enhanced liquidity protection does not have to be provided necessarily by the government: A private facility, adequately capitalized and financed by the MMF industry, could be set up to supply liquidity to funds that most need it at times of market stress. Depending on its structure, such a private facility itself might have access to broader liquidity backstops.

A private emergency liquidity facility could be beneficial on several levels. First, a private liquidity facility, in combination with the SEC's new liquidity requirements, might substantially buttress MMFs' ability to withstand outflows without selling assets in potentially illiquid markets.[18] Second, a private emergency facility might offer important efficiency gains from risk pooling. Even during the systemic liquidity crisis in 2008, individual MMFs experienced large variations in the timing and magnitude of redemptions. An emergency facility could provide liquidity to the MMFs that need it; in contrast, liquidity requirements for individual MMFs would likely leave some funds with too much liquidity and others with too little. Third, a private liquidity facility might provide funds with flexibility in managing liquidity risks if, for example, regulators allowed MMFs some relief in liquidity requirements in return for the funds' purchase of greater access to the liquidity facility's capacity.

---

[17] Outflows from prime MMFs totaled about $200 billion in the two days prior to the Treasury and Federal Reserve announcements on Friday, September 19, 2008. However, in the two business days following the announcements (Monday and Tuesday, September 22 and 23), outflows were just $22 billion.

[18] For example, as noted in the text, even if MMFs in September 2008 had held liquid assets in the proportions that the SEC has recently mandated, the net redemptions experienced by the funds following the Lehman Brothers bankruptcy would have forced MMFs to sell considerable amounts of securities into illiquid markets in the absence of the substantial government interventions. But a liquidity facility with the capacity to provide an additional 10 percent overnight liquidity to each fund would double the effective overnight liquid resources available to MMFs. If MMFs in September 2008 had already been in compliance with the new liquidity requirements, a facility with this capacity would have considerably reduced funds' need to raise liquidity (for example, through asset sales) during the run. In addition, the very existence of the facility might have reduced redemption requests in the first place.

Importantly, a properly designed and well-managed private liquidity facility would internalize the cost of liquidity protection for the MMF industry and provide appropriate incentives for MMFs and their investors.[19] Such a facility would not help funds that take on excessive capital risks or face runs because of isolated credit losses (a well-designed private liquidity facility would not have helped the Reserve Primary Fund or its shareholders avoid losses in September 2008 due to holdings of Lehman Brothers debt). Moreover, a liquidity facility alone may not prevent runs on MMFs triggered by concerns about more widespread credit losses at MMFs. However, a liquidity facility could substantially reduce the damage that a run on a single distressed fund might cause to the rest of the industry.

While a private emergency liquidity facility would be appealing in several respects, setting up an effective facility would present a number of challenges. The structure and operations of a private liquidity facility would have to be considered carefully to ensure that it would be effective during crises and that it would not unduly distort incentives, while, at the same time, that it would be in compliance with all applicable regulations and that it would not favor certain market participants or business models. For example:

- On the one hand, if MMFs were required to participate in a private facility, regulators would assume some responsibility for ensuring that the facility was operated equitably and efficiently, that it managed risks prudently, and that it was able to provide liquidity effectively during a crisis. On the other hand, if participation were voluntary, some MMFs would likely choose not to participate to avoid sharing in the costs associated with the facility. Non-participating MMFs might present greater risks than their competitors but would free-ride on the stability the liquidity facility would provide. In a voluntary participation framework, one means of balancing risks between MMFs that do and do not participate in a liquidity facility would be to require nonparticipants to adhere to more stringent risk-limiting constraints or to require such funds to switch to a floating NAV. Such an approach (in which some MMFs have stable NAVs and others floating NAVs) is considered in section 3(e).

- Ensuring that the facility has adequate capacity to meet MMFs' liquidity needs during a crisis would be critical to the effectiveness of the facility in mitigating systemic risk. Inadequate capacity might, for example, create an incentive for MMF advisers to tap the facility before others do and thus make the facility itself vulnerable to runs. News of a depleted liquidity facility might amplify investor concerns and trigger or expand a run on MMFs. However, raising enough capital to build adequate liquidity capacity without undue leverage would be a challenge for the asset management industry. Accordingly, meaningful mitigation of systemic risk may require that the facility itself have access to alternative sources of liquidity.

---

[19] A private liquidity facility could also result in retail fund investors bearing some of the costs of meeting the likely higher liquidity needs of institutional funds. Consideration should be given as to whether and how to prevent such an outcome.

- A private facility may face conflicts of interest during a crisis when liquidity is in short supply. Responsibility to the facility's shareholders would mandate prudence in providing liquidity to MMFs. For example, facility managers would want to be selective in providing liquidity against term commercial paper out of concern about losses on such paper. However, excessive prudence would be at odds with the facility serving as an effective liquidity backstop. In addition, a private facility may face conflicts among different types of shareholders and participants who may have different interests, and a strong governance structure would be needed to address these conflicts as well as prevent the domination of the facility by the advisers of larger funds.

- Rules governing access to the facility would have to be crafted carefully to minimize the moral hazard problems among fund advisers, who could face diminished incentives to maintain liquidity in their MMFs. However, excessive constraints on access would limit the facility's effectiveness. An appropriate balancing of access rules might be difficult to achieve.

Notwithstanding these concerns, a private emergency liquidity facility could play an important role in supplementing the SEC's new liquidity requirements for MMFs. The potential advantages and disadvantages of such a facility, as well as its optimal structure and modes of operation, should be the subjects of further analysis and discussion.

c. *Mandatory Redemptions in Kind*

When investors make large redemptions from MMFs, they impose liquidity costs on other shareholders in the fund. For example, redemptions may force a fund to sell its most liquid assets to raise cash. Remaining shareholders are left with claims on a less liquid portfolio, so redemptions are particularly costly for other shareholders during a crisis, when liquidity is most valued.[20]

A requirement that MMFs distribute large redemptions by institutional investors in kind, rather than in cash, would force these redeeming shareholders to bear their own liquidity costs and reduce their incentive to redeem.[21] If liquidity pressures are causing money market instruments to trade at discounts, a MMF that distributes a large redemption in cash may have to sell securities at a discount to raise the cash. All shareholders in the fund would share in the loss on a pro rata basis. However, if the fund distributes securities to the investor in proportion to the claim on the fund represented by

---

[20] The problem is exacerbated by a rounded NAV, because a fund that has already incurred a capital loss but that continues to redeem each share at $1 also transfers capital losses from redeeming shareholders to those who remain in the fund.

[21] Such a requirement also would force redeeming shareholders to bear their share of any losses that a MMF has already incurred—even if the fund maintains a stable, rounded NAV and has not yet broken the buck—rather than concentrating those losses entirely in the MMF and thus on remaining MMF shareholders.

the redeemed shares, the liquidity risk would be borne most directly by the redeeming investor. If the fund elects to dispose of the securities in a dislocated market and incurs a loss, other shareholders are not directly affected.[22]

Requiring large redemptions to be made in kind would reduce, but not eliminate the systemic risk associated with large, widespread redemptions. Shareholders with immediate liquidity needs who receive securities from MMFs would have to sell those assets, and the consequences for short-term markets of such sales would be similar to the effects if the money market fund itself had sold the securities. Smaller shareholders would still receive cash redemptions, and larger investors might structure their MMF investments and redemptions to remain under the in-kind threshold.

An in-kind redemption requirement would present some operational and policy challenges. Portfolio holdings of MMFs sometimes are not freely transferable or are only transferable in large blocks of shares, so delivery of an exact pro rata portion of each portfolio holding to a redeeming shareholder may be impracticable. Thus, a fund may have to deliver different securities to different investors but would need to do so in an equitable manner. Funds should not, for example, be able to distribute only their most liquid assets to redeeming shareholders, since doing so would undermine the purpose of an in-kind redemptions requirement. Thus, the SEC would have to make key judgments on the circumstances under which a fund must redeem in kind, as well as the criteria that funds would use for determining which portfolio securities must be distributed and how they would be valued.

d. *Insurance for MMFs*

As noted in section 1(b), the absence of formal capital buffers or insurance for MMFs, as well as their historical reliance on discretionary sponsor support in place of such mechanisms, further contributes to their vulnerability to runs. Treasury's Temporary Guarantee Program for Money Market Funds, announced on September 19, 2008, was a key component of the government intervention that slowed the run on MMFs. The program provided guarantees for shares in MMFs as of the announcement date. These guarantees were somewhat akin to deposit insurance, which for many decades has played a central role in mitigating the risk of runs on banks.[23] Therefore, some form of insurance for MMF shareholders might be helpful in mitigating systemic

---

[22] If the investor sells securities at a loss, however, and the MMF also holds the same or similar securities, the fund may be forced to re-price the securities and lower its mark-to-market, shadow NAV. So, remaining investors in the fund may be affected indirectly by the redeeming investor, even if that investor receives redemptions in kind.

[23] All publicly offered stable NAV MMFs were eligible to participate in the program. If a MMF elected to participate, the program guaranteed that each shareholder in that MMF would receive the stable share price (typically $1) for each share held in the fund, up to the number of shares held as of the close of business on September 19, 2008. In the event that a participating MMF broke the buck, the fund was required to suspend redemptions and commence liquidation, and the fund was eligible to collect payment from Treasury to enable payment of the stable share price to each covered investor. Treasury neither received any claims for payment nor incurred any losses under the program.

risks posed by MMFs, although insurance also may create new risks by distorting incentives of fund advisers and shareholders.

Like an external liquidity facility, insurance would reduce the risk of runs on MMFs, but the consequences of insurance and a liquidity facility would otherwise be different. A liquidity facility would do little or nothing to help a fund that had already experienced a capital loss, but such a facility might be very helpful in mitigating the destabilizing effects that one fund's capital loss might impose on the rest of the industry. Insurance, in contrast, would substantially reduce or eliminate any losses borne by the shareholders of the MMF that experienced the capital loss and damp their incentives to redeem shares in that fund. Although either option might reduce the incentives for asset managers and shareholders to minimize risks, a liquidity facility without an insurance scheme would leave intact shareholders' incentive to monitor funds for the credit and interest rate risks that may trigger a run. However, in a crisis that triggers concerns about widespread credit losses, liquidity protection without some form of insurance may still leave MMFs vulnerable to runs.

In addition to these general considerations, the design and implementation of an insurance program for MMFs would require resolution of a number of difficult issues. For example:

- Insurance could, in principle, be provided by the private sector, the government, or a combination of the two, but all three options have potential drawbacks. Private insurers have had considerable difficulties in fairly pricing and successfully guaranteeing rare but high-cost financial events, as demonstrated, for example, by the recent difficulties experienced by financial guarantors. That no private market for insurance has developed is some evidence that such insurance for MMFs may be a challenging business model, particularly if funds are not required to obtain insurance.[24] Making insurance for MMFs mandatory could attract private insurance providers, but the pricing and scope of coverage that these providers could offer would need to be the subject of careful consideration. In any case, insurers would need to maintain capital and carry reinsurance as necessary to cover losses during extraordinary events. Public insurance would necessitate new government oversight and administration functions and, particularly in the absence of private insurance, would require a mechanism for setting appropriate risk-based premiums (either pre- or post-event). A hybrid insurance scheme—for example, with MMFs or their

---

[24] The degree of insurance coverage provided by Treasury's Temporary Guarantee Program for Money Market Funds was unprecedented. Private insurance with considerably narrower coverage has been available to MMFs in the past: ICI Mutual Insurance Company, an industry association captive insurer, offered very limited insurance to MMFs from 1999 to 2003. This insurance covered losses on MMF portfolio assets due to defaults and insolvencies but not losses due to events such as a security downgrade or a rise in interest rates. Coverage was limited to $50 million per fund, with a deductible of the first 10 to 40 basis points of any loss. Premiums ranged from 1 to 3 basis points. ICI Mutual reportedly discontinued offering the insurance in 2003 because coverage restrictions and other factors limited demand to the point that the insurance was not providing enough risk pooling to remain viable. Of course, MMFs continue to have access to other market-based mechanisms for transferring risks, such as credit default swaps, although holdings of such derivative securities by MMFs are tightly regulated by rule 2a-7.

sponsors retaining the first level of losses up to a threshold, private insurers or risk pools handling losses up to a certain higher threshold, and a government insurance program serving as a backstop (perhaps with post-event recoupment)—might offer some advantages, but it would be subject to the risks of private insurance and the challenges of public insurance.

- On the one hand, mandatory participation in an insurance system likely would be necessary to instill investor confidence in the MMF industry, to ensure an adequate pooling of risk, to prevent riskier funds from opting out yet free-riding on the stability afforded by insured funds, and to create a sufficient premium base. On the other hand, an insurance requirement would create new government responsibilities, and the regulatory and economic implications of such a requirement would have to be evaluated carefully.

- Insurance increases moral hazard and would shift incentives for prudent risk management by MMFs from fund advisers, who are better positioned to monitor risks, to public or private insurers. In addition, insurance removes investors' incentives to monitor risk management by fund advisers. Broadly speaking, insurance fundamentally changes the nature of MMF shares, from pooled pass-through investments in risky assets to insured products with relatively low yields and limited or no risk.

- Appropriate pricing would be critical to the success of a MMF insurance program, as pricing would affect the financial position of the guarantor, the incentives of MMF advisers, and the relative attractiveness of different types of MMFs and their competitors (for example, bank deposits). Insurance pricing that is not responsive to the riskiness of individual MMF portfolios, for example, would heighten moral hazard problems that undermine incentives for prudent MMF risk management. Underpriced insurance might cause disruptive outflows from bank deposits to MMFs and would be a subsidy for sponsors of and investors in MMFs. Still, insurance for MMFs might be easier to price fairly than deposit insurance for banks, as MMF portfolios are highly restricted, relatively homogeneous in comparison with bank portfolios, transparent, and priced on a daily basis.

- Limits on insurance coverage (perhaps similar to those for deposit insurance) would be needed to avoid giving MMFs an advantage over banks and to preserve incentives for large investors to monitor the risk management practices at MMFs. However, such limits would leave most institutional investors' shares only marginally covered by insurance and do little to reduce their incentive to run should MMF risks become salient.

e. *A Two-Tier System of MMFs, with Enhanced Protections for Stable NAV MMFs*

Reforms intended to reduce the systemic risks posed by MMFs might be particularly effective if they allow investors some flexibility in choosing the MMFs that best match their risk-return preferences. Policymakers might accommodate a range of preferences by allowing two types of MMFs to be regulated under rule 2a-7:

(i) Stable NAV MMFs. These funds would continue to maintain stable, rounded NAVs, but they would be subject to enhanced protections, which might include some combination of tighter regulation (such as higher liquidity standards) and required access to an external liquidity backstop. Other options to provide enhanced protection for stable NAV funds might include mandatory distribution of large redemptions in kind and insurance. (Policymakers may also consider limiting the risk arising from investors in stable NAV funds by restricting sales of such funds' shares to retail investors, as discussed in section 3(f).)

(ii) Floating NAV funds. Although these MMFs would still have to comply with many of the current restrictions of rule 2a-7, these restrictions might be somewhat less stringent than those for stable NAV funds. So, floating NAV funds could bear somewhat greater credit and liquidity risks than stable NAV funds, might not be required to obtain access to external sources of liquidity or insurance, and most likely would pay higher yields than their stable NAV counterparts. Regulatory relief—for example, allowing simplified tax treatment for small NAV changes in funds that adhere to rule 2a-7—might help preserve the attractiveness of such funds for many investors.

A two-tier system could mitigate the systemic risks that arise from a stable, rounded NAV, by requiring funds that maintain a stable NAV to have additional protections that directly address some of the features that contribute to their vulnerability to runs. At the same time, by preserving stable NAV funds, such a system would mitigate the risks of a wholesale shift to floating NAV funds. For example, a two-tier system would diminish the likelihood of a large-scale exodus from the MMF industry by investors who might find a floating NAV MMF unacceptable.

Floating NAV MMFs would face a lower risk of runs for the reasons outlined in section 3(a): Frequent changes in these funds' NAVs would help align investor perceptions and actual fund risks, and investors would have reduced incentives to redeem early in a crisis without a rounded NAV. In addition, investor sorting might ameliorate the risk of runs: Under such a two-tier system, investors who choose floating NAV funds presumably would be less risk-averse and more tolerant of NAV changes than the shareholders of stable NAV funds.

During a crisis, investors would likely shift at least some assets from riskier floating NAV MMFs to stable NAV MMFs, which would presumably be safer because of their enhanced protections. Such flows might be similar, in some respects, to the asset flows seen during the September 2008 crisis from prime MMFs to government MMFs, but a shift between tiers of prime funds could be less disruptive to short-term funding markets and the aggregate supply of credit to private firms than a flight from prime to government MMFs. Effective design of a two-tier system would have to incorporate measures to ensure that large-scale shifts of assets among MMFs in crises would not be disruptive.[25]

For a two-tier system to be effective and materially mitigate the risk of runs, investors would have to fully understand the difference between the two types of funds and their associated risks. Investors who do not make this distinction might flee indiscriminately from floating NAV and stable NAV funds alike; in this case, a two-tier system would not be effective in mitigating the risk of runs.

The relative ease or difficulty of implementing a two-tier system would depend on the nature of the stable NAV and floating NAV MMFs that comprise it. For example, if the stable NAV funds simply were required to satisfy more stringent SEC rules governing portfolio safety, creation of a two-tier system would be fairly straightforward. A requirement that stable NAV funds obtain access to an emergency liquidity facility would likely make stable NAV funds less prone to runs and would reduce the likelihood that investors flee indiscriminately from both types of funds in the event of severe market strains. However, this approach also would face the challenges associated with the creation of an effective liquidity facility (discussed in more detail in section 3(b)).

f. A Two-Tier System of MMFs, with Stable NAV MMFs Reserved for Retail Investors

Another approach to the two-tier system described in section 3(e) could distinguish stable NAV and floating NAV funds by investor type. Stable NAV MMFs could be made available only to retail investors, while institutional investors would be restricted to floating NAV funds.

This approach would bring enhanced protections to stable NAV MMFs by mitigating the risk arising from the behavior of their investors, because institutional investors have historically generated greater risks of runs for MMFs than retail investors. As noted previously, the run from MMFs in September 2008 was primarily a flight by institutional investors. More than 90 percent of the net outflows from prime MMFs in the week following the Lehman Brothers bankruptcy came from institutional funds, and institutional investors withdrew substantial sums from prime MMFs even before the Reserve Primary Fund broke the buck.

Moreover, evidence suggests that the additional risks posed by institutional investors during the run on MMFs in September 2008 were not unique to that episode. Relative to retail investors, institutional investors have greater resources to monitor MMF portfolios and risks and have larger amounts at stake, and are therefore quicker to redeem

---

[25] If stable NAV MMFs carried mandatory insurance, some limitations on insurance coverage (for example, stipulating that individual shares in such funds could be insured only after a given number of days) might reduce the magnitude of flows between different types of MMFs and reduce implicit subsidies for investors who purchase shares in stable NAV funds only during crises. However, such rules might diminish the value of insurance in preventing runs.

shares on concerns about MMF risks. Institutional MMFs typically have greater cash flow volatility than retail funds. Net flows to institutional MMFs have also exhibited patterns indicating that institutional investors regularly arbitrage small discrepancies between MMFs' shadow NAVs and their $1 share prices.[26] These observations suggest that many institutional investors are aware of such discrepancies—which are likely to widen during financial crises—and are able to exploit them.

A two-tier system based on investor type would protect the interests of retail investors by reducing the likelihood that a run might begin in institutional MMFs (as it did in September 2008) and spread to retail funds. Moreover, such a system would preserve the original purpose of MMFs, which was to provide retail investors with cost-effective access to diversified investments in money market instruments. Retail investors have few alternative opportunities to obtain such exposures. In contrast, institutional investors, which can meet minimum investment thresholds for direct investments in money market instruments, would be able to continue doing so.

One advantage of this alternative is that it could be accomplished by SEC rulemaking under existing authorities without establishing additional market structures. A prohibition on institutional investors' use of stable NAV MMFs would have some practical hurdles, however. Successful enforcement of the rule would require the SEC to define who would qualify as retail and institutional investors. In practice, such distinctions may be difficult, although not impossible, to make. For example, retail investors who own MMF shares because of their participation in defined contribution plans (such as 401(k) plans) may be invested in institutional MMFs through omnibus accounts that are overseen by institutional investors (plan administrators). Simple rules that might be used to identify institutional investors, such as defining as institutional any investor whose account size exceeds a certain threshold, would be imperfect and could motivate the use of workarounds (such as brokered accounts) by institutional investors. The SEC, as part of its rulemaking, would need to take steps to prevent such workarounds.

Because many institutional investors may be particularly unwilling to switch to floating NAV MMFs, a prohibition on sales of stable NAV MMFs shares to such investors may have many of the same unintended consequences as a requirement that all MMFs adopt floating NAVs (see section 3(a)). In particular, prohibiting institutional investors from holding stable NAV funds might cause large shifts in assets to unregulated MMF substitutes. This concern is of particular importance given that institutional MMFs currently account for almost two-thirds of the assets under management in MMFs.

In addition, a two-tier system based on investor type would preclude some of the advantages of allowing institutional investors to choose between stable NAV MMFs and floating NAV MMFs (as the option described in section 3(e) would permit). For example, under the two-tier system described in section 3(e), investor sorting would provide some protection for the floating NAV funds, because institutional investors

---

[26] For example, after Federal Open Market Committee (FOMC) actions that lower the FOMC's target for the federal funds rate, MMF shadow NAVs rise and institutional MMFs often experience large net inflows.

holding floating NAV MMFs likely would be less risk-averse than those who held stable NAV funds. With institutional investors prohibited from holding shares in stable NAV MMFs, such sorting among these investors would not occur. During a crisis, under the system described in section 3(e), institutional investors might be expected to shift assets from floating NAV MMFs to stable NAV funds, but a ban on institutional holdings of stable NAV MMF shares would prevent such shifts.

g. Regulating Stable NAV MMFs as Special Purpose Banks.

Functional similarities between MMF shares and deposits, as well as the risk of runs on both types of instruments, provide a rationale for introducing bank-like regulation for MMFs. For example, mandating that stable NAV MMFs be reorganized as SPBs might subject these MMFs to banking oversight and regulation, including requirements for reserves and capital buffers, and provide MMFs with access to a liquidity backstop and insurance coverage within a regulatory framework specifically designed for mitigation of systemic risk.[27] If each MMF were offered the option of implementing a floating NAV as an alternative to reorganizing as a bank, the reorganization requirement for stable NAV MMFs might be viewed as part of a two-tier system for MMFs.[28]

Although the conceptual basis for converting stable NAV MMFs to SPBs is seemingly straightforward, in practice this option spans a broad range of possible implementations, most of which would require legislative changes and complex interagency regulatory coordination. The advantages and disadvantages of this reform option depend on how exactly the conversion to SPBs would be implemented and how the new banks would be structured. A thorough discussion of the full range of possibilities—including their feasibility, probable effect on the MMF industry, broader implications for the banking system, and likely efficacy in mitigating systemic risk—would be quite complex and is beyond the scope of this report.

As an example of the issues that this option involves, one possible approach to its implementation would be to preserve stable NAV MMFs as standalone entities but to treat their shares as deposits for the purposes of banking law. These shares, unlike other deposits, might be claims specifically (and only) on MMF assets, which could continue to be subject to strict risk-limiting regulations such as those provided by rule 2a-7 or similar rules. The introduction of such hybrid investment vehicles would preserve investors' opportunity to benefit from mutualized investments in private money market instruments,

---

[27] Such an approach to MMF reform was advocated by the Group of Thirty. See Group of Thirty, *Financial Reform: A Framework for Financial Stability*, released on January 15, 2009.

[28] There may be a question as to whether floating NAV MMFs—if such funds are offered—should or should not be required to reorganize as SPBs. Other mutual funds with floating NAVs, such as ultra-short bond funds, presumably would not be affected by a mandate that MMFs reorganize as SPBs. The principal distinction between other (non-MMF) mutual funds and floating NAV MMFs would be that the latter are constrained by rule 2a-7 and thus have less risky portfolios, so the advantages and disadvantages of mandating these funds to reorganize as banks would have to be carefully evaluated. However, policymakers could consider prohibiting floating NAV MMFs from offering bank-like services that attract risk-averse investors, such as the ability to provide transactions services.

but, being a novel combination of features of banks and mutual funds, such vehicles would also present complex regulatory and operational challenges. In contrast, other approaches to converting MMFs to SPBs, such as absorbing or transforming stable NAV MMFs into financial institutions that offer traditional deposits, might be simpler to accomplish in practice, but nonetheless subject to different sets of challenges. In particular, if the deposits offered by the new SPBs were only of the types currently offered by other banks, investors—and particularly retail investors, who have few alternative opportunities to obtain diversified exposures to money market instruments—would lose access to important investment options.[29] In addition, to the extent that banks have different preferences for portfolio assets than MMFs, a simple transformation of MMFs into depository institutions might lead to a decline in the availability of short-term financing for firms and state and local governments that currently rely on money markets to satisfy their funding needs. Considerable further study would thus be needed in pursuing this option.

Leaving aside the details of how exactly this option could be implemented, in general terms, a principal advantage of reorganizing MMFs as SPBs is that such a change would provide MMFs with a broad regulatory framework similar to existing regulatory systems that are designed for mitigation of systemic risk. Investments in MMFs and insured deposits—which already serve some similar functions, particularly for retail investors—could be regulated similarly. MMFs and their investors might benefit from access to government insurance and emergency liquidity facilities at a price similar to that currently paid by depository institutions. Importantly, such access would not require any extraordinary government actions (such as the establishment in September 2008 of Treasury's Temporary Guarantee Program for Money Market Funds or the creation of the Federal Reserve's AMLF); instead, the terms of such access would be codified and well-understood in advance.

Moreover, by providing explicit capital buffers, access to a liquidity backstop, and deposit insurance, a conversion of stable NAV MMFs to SPBs might substantially reduce the uncertainties and systemic risks associated with MMF sponsors' current practice of discretionary capital support. Clear rules for how the buffers, backstop, and insurance would be used would improve the transparency of the allocation of risks among market participants.

However, the capital needed to reorganize MMFs as SPBs may be a significant hurdle to successful implementation of this option. Access to the Federal Reserve discount window and deposit insurance coverage most likely would require that the new SPBs hold reservable deposits and meet specific capitalization standards.[30] Given the

---

[29] In contrast, institutional investors could continue to obtain such exposures either by investing directly in money market instruments or by holding shares in offshore MMFs, enhanced cash funds, and other stable value vehicles. Hence, absorption of MMFs by banks might have the unintended effect of reducing investment opportunities for retail investors, who generally did not participate in the run on MMFs in 2008, while leaving money market investment options for institutional investors largely intact.

[30] Currently, MMFs are essentially 100 percent capital—their liabilities are the equity shares held by investors—so the meaning of "capital requirements" for such funds is not clear. However, if MMFs were reorganized as SPBs, their capital structure would become more complex. MMF shares would likely be

scale of assets under management in the MMF industry, MMF sponsors (or banks) that wish to keep funds operating would have to raise substantial equity—probably at least tens of billions of dollars—to meet regulatory capital requirements.[31] Raising such sums would be a considerable challenge. The asset management business typically is not capital intensive, so many asset managers—and several of the largest sponsors of MMFs—are lightly capitalized and probably could not provide such amounts of capital. If asset managers or other firms were unwilling or unable to raise the capital needed to operate the new SPBs, a sharp reduction in assets in stable NAV MMFs might diminish their capacity to supply short-term credit, curtail the availability of an attractive investment option (particularly for retail investors), and motivate institutional investors to shift assets to unregulated vehicles.

An additional hurdle to converting MMFs to SPBs would be the substantial increase in explicit government guarantees that would result from the creation of new insured deposits. The potential liability to the government probably would far exceed any premiums that could be collected for some time.

Uncertainties about the reaction of institutional investors to MMFs reorganized as SPBs raise some important concerns about whether such reorganizations would provide a substantial degree of systemic-risk mitigation. Coverage limits on deposit insurance would leave many large investors unprotected in case of a significant capital loss. Thus, even with the protections afforded to banks, MMFs would still be vulnerable to runs by institutional investors, unless much higher deposit insurance limits were allowed for the newly created SPBs. Moreover, even in the absence of runs, institutional MMFs often experience volatile cash flows, and the potential effects of large and high-frequency flows into and out of the banking system (if MMFs become SPBs) would need to be analyzed carefully.

The reaction of institutional investors to the altered set of investment opportunities may also have unintended consequences. For example, SPBs that pay positive net yields to investors (depositors) would be very attractive for institutional investors who currently cannot receive interest on traditional bank deposits.[32] Thus, on the one hand, the new SPBs might prompt shifts of assets by institutional investors from the traditional banking system. On the other hand, a substantial mandatory capital buffer for MMFs would reduce their net yields and possibly motivate institutional investors to move assets from MMFs to unregulated alternatives (particularly if regulatory reform does not include new constraints on such vehicles). The effect of these competing

---

converted to deposit liabilities, and MMFs would have to hold additional capital (equity) buffers to absorb first losses. Capital requirements would regulate the size of such buffers.

[31] The magnitude of the capital required might be reduced if floating NAV MMFs were not required to reorganize as SPBs and if a substantial number of funds elected to float their NAVs rather than reorganize as banks. In addition, the capital required might be reduced somewhat if regulators determined that the nature of the assets held by MMFs justifies capital requirements that are lower than those imposed on commercial banks and thrifts.

[32] Section 627 of the Dodd-Frank Act repeals the prohibition on banks paying interest on corporate demand deposit accounts effective July 21, 2011.

incentives on institutional investors' cash management practices is uncertain, but it is at least plausible that a reorganization of MMFs as SPBs may lead to a net shift of assets to unregulated investment vehicles.

h. Enhanced Constraints on Unregulated MMF Substitutes

New rules intended to reduce the susceptibility of MMFs to runs generally also will reduce the appeal of the funds to many investors. For example, several of the reforms recently adopted by the SEC probably will reduce the net yields that the funds pay to shareholders, and a switch to floating NAVs would eliminate a feature that some MMF shareholders see as essential.

Reforms that reduce the appeal of MMFs may motivate some institutional investors to move assets to alternative cash management vehicles with stable NAVs, such as offshore MMFs, enhanced cash funds, and other stable value vehicles. These vehicles typically invest in the same types of short-term instruments that MMFs hold and share many of the features that make MMFs vulnerable to runs, so growth of unregulated MMF substitutes would likely increase systemic risks. However, such funds need not comply with rule 2a-7 or other ICA protections and in general are subject to little or no regulatory oversight. In addition, the risks posed by MMF substitutes are difficult to monitor, since they provide far less market transparency than MMFs.

Thus, effective mitigation of systemic risks may require policy reforms targeted outside the MMF industry to address risks posed by funds that compete with MMFs and to combat regulatory arbitrage that might offset intended reductions in MMF risks. Such reforms most likely would require legislation and action by the SEC and other agencies. For example, consideration should be given to prohibiting unregistered investment vehicles from maintaining stable NAVs, perhaps by amending sections 3(c)(1) and 3(c)(7) of the ICA to specify that exemptions from the requirement to register as an investment company do not apply to funds that seek a stable NAV. Banking and state insurance regulators might consider additional restrictions to mitigate systemic risk for bank common and collective funds and other investment pools that seek a stable NAV but that are exempt from registration under sections 3(c)(3) and 3(c)(11) of the ICA.

www.ingramcontent.com/pod-product-compliance
Lightning Source LLC
Chambersburg PA
CBHW081807170526
45167CB00008B/3358